Finding W :
The Great
Alphabet Hunt

Paula Curtis Taylorson

illustrated by Jessica Palmer

Finding W : The Great Alphabet Hunt

This is a work of fiction.

Library of Congress Control Number: 2021905046

Printed in the United States of America

A 2 Z Press LLC

PO Box 582

Deleon Springs, FL 32130

bestlittleonlinebookstore.com

sizemore3630@aol.com

440-241-3126

ISBN: 978-1-954191-24-2

This book belongs to

Dedication

Thank you to those who read to me and those who listened to me read.

On his **way** around the **world**,
his eyes are open **wide**,

taking lots of pictures **with**
Waldo wombat by his side.

One **wintery**, **Wednesday** morning, as the **wind** blew **wild** and **wet**, they packed up their **whacky** four-**wheeled** drive and off they set.

And checking out their **wrinkled** map, to see **which way** to go, they stopped and asked a **wildcat** to see if she **would** know!

Heading **west** along **Wichita** highway,
they passed the Texas **waterfall**.
Walter pulled over and parked
beside a **whitewashed wall**.

WITCHITA HWY
TEXAS FALLS

Waterlilies surround
a **whopping weeping willow** tree,
where a family of **wildfowl**
and **weaverbirds** ate
walnut cake for tea!

Walter took a photo
and **walked** on up the hill,

He followed a **wiggly, winding** path to a **wooden, wrecked** windmill.

A wobbly 'WELCOME' sign was nailed willy-nilly to a **wrought** iron door,

When Walt and Waldo knocked loudly, they **were** greeted by **Wilbur**, a **winsome, wonky** boar.

Wilbur gave them **watermelon** and **waffles** to eat along the **way**. **Wandering** back to their jeep, they **wished** that they could stay.

Then **Wilbur whistled** loudly
and in a **wink** of his eye,
he **willingly** posed for the camera
as he **waved** to them goodbye.

Weaving back down the mountain, they saw **Wendy**, a **wholesome weasel**. She **wore** a **wetsuit** and a **wide-brimmed** hat painting **wispy watercolours** on an easel.

Some **wayward warthogs wallowed** in mud
and splashed it **wildly** on their faces.
It **was** time for **Walter** and **Waldo**
to visit other **well-known** places!

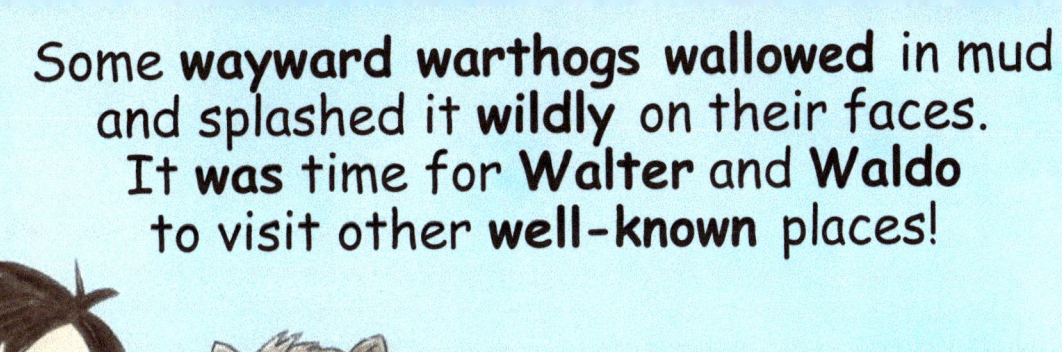

So off to **Washington** D.C. to the **Whitehouse**, a great place to be seen. **Where** the President's cat, combed his **whiskers** **while watching** his clothes **whirl** around in the **washing** machine.

Snapping away **with** the camera they **wait**, stuck in traffic at Capital Hill.

Wilber and Wombat at the Whitehouse

The police **whooshed** by them in a hurry, so they decided to fly off to Brazil!

At the top of Sugarloaf Mountain,
stood a **wolf who was wily and witty**.
He sold **watches, wristbands, wellington**
boots and postcards with views of the city.

FOR SALE $5
*Watches   *Wellingtons
*Wristbands   *Postcards

'Come closer,' he said **wryly** to **Waldo**, **we'll** do a selfie and then **we'll** have a quick snack.

Waldo was wise for a wombat and said warmly,

'Can you wait a while? I'll be back?'

At a chapel close by, **worthy women wore wigs** bought at **weekend** sales. Two **whimsical whippets witnessed** a **wedding, wearing** rings on their **wee, wagging** tails.

The best man was a **wildebeest** called **Wes**. He **wore** a **waistcoat** of **wildflowers**. He **whispered**, 'The bridesmaids look **wonderful**,' then **waltzed with** them for hours.

It **was** time to move on for more snapshots
of **white waves** and golden sand,

at the **well-cared** for beaches of Waikiki,
where the not-so-**wimpy wasps** often land.

A **weighty walrus** from **western** Samoa **was wading** on his back, catching a tan.

Suddenly, he **was wrapped** up in a sail as a **wallaby windsurfer** spun like a fan.

In a **warehouse west** of **Wadua**, in Sri Lanka, a **whirring** noise could be heard. **Walter went** in close for a photo of this **whiny** sounding bird.

Sneaking a peek through a **window**, the **wishful Wright** brothers **were** fixing their plane. **While** a **woodpecker** sat high on a **wire**, watching wiggling worms playing a game.

A **wizard** who **wanted** to be helpful, offered
to **whizz** them to **Wong Tai** in Hong Kong.
His **wand was** a **wurst** sausage
from **Weimar,** but his spell **went** horribly **wrong!**

Walter and Waldo ended up locked in a **wardrobe**, **where** some **weevils** helped them get loose.

Then, they **were** stuck in **Warsaw**, Poland with a **woodlouse** **who** sold **wheatgrass** and **watercress** juice.

Searching **worldwide** for **W's** is challenging,
but **Walter** and **Waldo** did it indeed.
If you are **willing** to put in some hard **work,**
it is so **worthwhile when** you succeed!

My Very Own 'W' Words:

_____

_____

_____

_____

_____

_____

_____

_____

_____

_____

_____

Glossary

Page 1. **Wildlife** : animals that live in the wild outdoors
Wondrous : wonderful, remarkable, marvelous
Walter : a boy or man's name
Will : someone or something that is about to or going to do something
W : a letter Also on page 1. : **Water bottle** : a container for water or other liquids
Wallet : a flat folding pocketbook to hold items

Page 2. **Way** : a method, plan, or means to obtaining a goal or doing something, a path
World : the Earth, or globe, the planet
Wide : a big opening side to side
Also on page 2. : **Whale** : a large mammal that lives in the sea water

Page 3. **With** : together
Waldo : the wombat's name here, male name
Wombat : any of several stocky, burrowing, plant-eating marsupials of of Australia the size of a badger

Page 4. **Wintery** : pertaining to the Winter season
Wednesday : a day of the week
Wind : air in natural motion, as that moving horizontally at any speed along the earth's surface
Wild : living in a state of nature; not tamed or domesticated, growing or produced without cultivation or the care of humans,
Wet : moistened, covered, or soaked with water or some other liquid
Whacky : odd or irrational; crazy
Four-**wheeled** drive : an automobile that drives with all four wheels and not less
Also on page 4.: **Watch** : jewelry to tell time
Wellington boots : rubber boots

Page 5. **Wrinkled** : not smooth, creased
Which : pertaining to a particular thing
Way : a path or a method of doing something
Wildcat : a cat that lives outside in the wild
Would : able to do or know something
Also on page 5.: **Watermelon** : fruit, food

Page 6. **West** : a direction
Wichita : a city in Kansas, USA
Waterfall : a steep fall or flow of water in a watercourse
from a height, as over a precipice; cascade
Whitewashed : covered in white paint or any white substance
Wall : a barrier made of wood, cement, glass
Also on page 6: **Wishing well** : a round well for
children to toss coins into to make a wish

Page 7. **Waterlilies** : plants that grow on the top of water
Whopping : large
Weeping willow : a tree with low flowing branches
Where : a particular place or circumstance
Wildfowl : birds that live in the wild and not in captivity
Weaverbirds : any of numerous African and Asian
finchlike birds noted for their elaborately
woven nests and colonial habits
Walnut : food

Page 8. **Walked** : to travel by foot

Page 9. **Wiggly** : wavy, not strait
Winding : something that is not strait,
many curves and turns are present
Wooden : something made with wood
Wrecked : damaged
Windmill : any of various machines for grinding,
pumping, and more driven by the force of the wind
acting upon a number of vanes or sails

Page 10. **Wobbly** : shaky; unsteady
Welcome: a word of kindly greeting
Willy-nilly : haphazard, disorganized
Wrought : light weight metal that resembles wood
Also on page 10. : **Wheelbarrow** : a large wheeled
bucket-like piece of equipment to carry items
Wildflowers : flowers that grow without care

Page 11. **When** : at a certain time or occasion
Were : something that happened (were greeted)
Wilbur : a boy or man's name
Winsome : charming in a childish way
Wonky : shaky, something not quite right

Page 12. **Watermelon** : a delicious, sweet fruit
Waffles : food
Wandering : to go without a purpose, roam, stray
Wished : to want; desire; long for

Page 13. **Whistled** : to make a clear musical sound
Wink : a quick closing of the eye or passage of time
Willingly : voluntarily, without force
Waved : to move in a large fashion

Page 14. **Weaving** : going back and forth,
not in a strait line
Wendy : a girl or woman's name
Wholesome : something healthy, good character
Weasel : any small carnivore with a long, slender
body and feeding chiefly on small rodents
Wore : to carry or have on the body or about
the person as a covering, equipment, ornament
Wetsuit : a special suit worn to keep
one warm in cold water
Wide-brimmed : very large brim on the hat here
Wispy : thin, delicate strokes of painting here
Watercolours : painted mixed with water to use of art

Page 15. **Wayward** – turned from right behavior
Warthogs : an African wild swine, with large tusks and warty protuberances on the face
Wallowed : to roll about or lie in water, snow, mud, dust, or the like, as for refreshment
Wildly : in a bizarre manner
Well-known : familiar, most are aware of

Page 16. **Washington** D.C. : a city, area where the government is in the USA
Whitehouse : the house where the President, the leader in the USA, works
Whiskers : the long hairs on the face of a cat
Watching : to sit and see something
Whirl : move around and around
Washing : to clean something, clothes here

Page 17. **Wait** : to remain inactive or in a state of repose, as until something expected happens

Page 18. **Whooshed** : to move quickly, a loud, rushing noise, as of air or water

Wilber and Wombat at the Whitehouse

Page 19. **Wolf** : an animal resembling a wild dog
Who : referring to a particular person
Wily : crafty, cunning
Witty : amusingly clever in perception and expression
Watches : a device to telling time worn on the lower arm
Wristbands : jewelry or fabric worn on the lower arm
Wellington boots : rubber boots

Page 20. **Wryly** : devious not truthful, crooked
We'll : a contracted word, we will

Page 21. **Wise** : having the power of discerning and judging properly as to what is true or right, possessing discernment, judgment, or discretion
Warmly : with kindness or gentle

Page 22. **Worthy** : valuable, excellent
Women : an adult female person
Wore : to put clothing or jewelry or make-up on one's body or face

Wigs : artificial hair
Weekend : days – Saturday and Sunday
Whimsical : erratic; unpredictable, fanciful notions
Whippets : dogs
Witnessed : to see, hear, or know by personal presence and perception, to be present at (an occurrence) as a formal witness, spectator, bystander

Wedding : the ceremony, event, where two people are married
Wearing : something put on someone
Wee : small
Wagging : to move back and forth

Page 23. **Wildebeest** : a gnu, a stocky, oxlike antelope from South African that is now protected
Wes : the name of a boy or man
Waistcoat : a vest, clothing
Wildflowers : the flower of a plant that normally grows in fields, forests, etc., without deliberate cultivation
Whispered : talk softly
Wonderful : excellent; great; marvelous, amazing, astonishing
Waltzed : dancing

Page 24. **White** : a color
Waves : the rising and falling of water in the sea

25 **Well-cared** : carefully looked after and tended to
Wimpy : timid or shy person or creature
Wasps : small insects with stingers that resemble bees

26 **Weighty** : important, heavy, big stuff
Walrus : a large sea creature resembling a seal
Western : pertaining to the West direction, the characteristics of western people
Wading : to walk through water, snow, sand, or any other substance that impedes free motion or offers resistance to movement, to play or in water when partially immersed

27 **Wrapped** : to enclose in something wound or folded about
Wallaby : any of various small and medium-sized kangaroos, some of which are no larger than rabbits, several species are endangered
Windsurfer : a form of sailing in which a flexible sail, free to move in any direction, is mounted on a surfboard and the craft guided by the standing rider

28 **Warehouse** : a large building to store things in
West : a direction
Wadua : a town in a country Sir Lanka
Whirring : to go, fly, revolve, or otherwise move quickly with a humming or buzzing sound
Whiny : sad complaining tone of voice

29 Window : an opening to see through or for things to pass through

Wishful : to want something strongly

Wright brothers : Orville and Wilbur, the brothers who were pioneer inventors in flying planes

Woodpecker : a bird with a large beak that pecks wood

Wire : a slender, stringlike piece or filament of relatively rigid or flexible metal, usually circular in section, manufactured in a great variety of diameters and metals depending on its application.

Wriggling : to move in all directions without order

Worms : long, legless creatures that live in the ground

30 Wizard : a magician who does magic

Wanted : to need or desire something, wish for something

Whizz : to move quickly

Wong Tai : a city in Hong Kong, China

Wand : a slim stick or rod for doing magic

Wurst sausage : food

Weimar : a city in Germany

Went : to do something here

Wrong : to have something happen that is not expected or correct

31 Wardrobe : a large piece of furniture for clothing

Weevils : an insect, a beetle

32 Warsaw : a city in Poland

Woodlouse : a small insect with a flat body

Wheatgrass : grass used for food, drinking

Watercress : leaves used in salads and drinks and soups

33 Worldwide : spanning the whole Earth

Willing : ready and eager to do something

Work : exert energy to accomplish something

Worthwhile : something for someone to find happy to do

Paula Curtis-Taylorson Lives in Marston Mortaine England. She is a full-time secondary school teacher of English and English Literature. She was amongst the first of the initial students to graduate from the Uk's first BA (Hons) Creative Writing Program at the University of Bedfordshire.

Her first love is poetry and rhyme and she works hard to inspire and teach appreciation of the subject to all age groups. Many of her students have gone on to be successful writers.